The Sacred Art of Letting Go

Walk 12 Steps with Spiritual Masters to
Let Go of Past Relationships and Find Peace Today

By Vishnu of Vishnu's Virtues

Copyright © 2019 Vishnu of Vishnu's Virtues
All rights reserved

"People have a hard time letting go of their suffering. Out of a fear of the unknown, they prefer suffering that is familiar." Thic Nhat Hanh

For weekly posts on letting go and starting over + for a free guide on opening your heart, visit http://www.vishnusvirtues.com/free-guide/

Contents

Dukkha (Suffering) 1

1. The Step of Acceptance 7
2. The Step of Release 17
3. The Step of Melting Anger 23
4. The Step of Choice 29
5. The Step of Learning 39
6. The Step of Connectedness 47
7. The Step of This Moment 53
8. The Step of Going Within 57
9. The Step of Soul Awakening 63
10. The Step of Compassion 69
11. The Step of Strength 75
12. The Step of Trust 81

Aarti (light) 87

References 93

About the Author 96

Dukkha (Suffering)

"Out of suffering have emerged the strongest souls; the most massive characters are seared with scars." Khalil Gibran

Your life is on hold.

You're stuck in the past.

The relationship you have been in for the last 10 years has come to a crashing halt.

Maybe one day your husband says he's not happy being married and wants to be single again.

Or, worse, he tells you that he's dating someone in another country and wants to have the freedom to be alone again.

You may have kids, a house and financial commitments but when a partner abandons it all for something that seems immature and sudden, you have no idea how to handle it.

It doesn't have to be some long-term marriage with commitments, either. You could have been with someone whom you were expecting to marry but this person had another idea in mind. Maybe he was afraid of a long-term commitment or maybe he just wanted to pursue his dreams.

Relationships come and go in our lives. After a particularly heart-breaking or soul-crushing relationship, people often tell you to "get over it."

But what I asked when my own marriage unraveled and divorce happened was: How exactly do you let go? It's not as easy as they say.

For the mentally strong and emotionally resilient, letting go is easy. It seems like some people jump out of bed in the morning, say "c'est la vie," and move on with their lives. They return to their morning routine, their workday and exercise routine, and live like nothing happened. They are a little sad but it's nothing a few episodes of "Stranger Things" can't cure.

If this is you, this book likely isn't for you.

I'm speaking to you, the sensitive soul, who tried to show up and do good in the world, then experienced heartbreak at the hands of someone else. All you wanted to do was love, give and put your all into a relationship. All you got in return was devastating heartbreak and a painful loss.

I'm here with you because I've been where you are. I went through heart-wrenching, gut-churning, soul-crunching heartbreak that left me paralyzed and heartbroken for years.

I simply could not move on.

I could not get out of bed.

I could not find peace.

I'm ashamed to say this but in the darkest moments of life after the breakup, I thought I wanted life itself to end because I couldn't see a life after the divorce.

I couldn't see any hope. I never thought I could get back in a relationship.

I believed I had let her down (even though she had initiated the divorce). I believed I had let both of our families down. I had let myself down.

So for the next several years, I decided to punish myself and hold myself accountable. I died in a way and became a ghost, living an existence in an alternative world.

I gave up my job, my career as a lawyer, a business I was running, the house I was living in.

So much fell apart when my marriage fell apart.

I had no motivation or hope of moving on. I thought to myself: 'What is the point of it all?'

I couldn't see myself in another relationship in the future and I couldn't imagine even wanting one.

For the next several years, I struggled with the pain of heartbreak and loss.

I reveled in the heartbreak. You know why? Not because it was painful and full of suffering. It was because I found familiarity in the pain and heartbreak. It was a place I knew well. Essentially, I substituted my heartbreak for my marriage. I chose something familiar (heartbreak and memories) to replace something else that was familiar (my relationship with my ex).

Why?

In this place of pain and heartbreak, suffering and loss, I had certainty. I could hold my memories close and relive the good times of the past. I could reflect on and fully absorb my pain, which was familiar and certain.

In loss, there is certainty and in that certainty, there is comfort.

You can hold onto your past because your past is like hot chicken soup or your favorite teddy bear from your childhood.

Even if the relationship is over, you can repeatedly think about the memories. You can open Facebook or your iPhone and endlessly reminisce about the beauty of your relationship. You can fall asleep each night remembering all the good times you had with your ex and the life you were dreaming of together.

In your mind, you don't have to let go. You can hold onto this relationship like your favorite blanket or most delicious comfort food. Holding on tightly to your past relationship will prevent you from having to face the pain of the unknown.

If you don't let go, you don't have to grieve, wallow in suffering, or fully experience the pain of heartbreak.

Like Thic Nhat Hahn said in the opening quote, you and I prefer suffering that is familiar.

What we can't stand is the unknown.

So, what are you to do if your husband walked out on you? What are you to do if your wife wants a divorce and is already moving in with someone else? What if the person you were going to marry changes their mind? The long-term relationship crumbles via a series of text messages?

You're facing something you've never faced before and feeling way outside your comfort zone.

The tears won't stop and the pain won't go away.

You might feel like you need a surgery to remove the gunshot wound or the sharp object that sliced and diced your heart.

I wrote this book to share my journey to recovery and also to challenge you to start your own journey.

You might not admit it but your pain and suffering might be too comfortable. And you might not realize it but being stuck in this yucky place of pain and discomfort might soothe your soul. Unfortunately, this familiar place of suffering is preventing you from moving on and living the life that's out there for you.

If you're stuck in the past or clutching your heartbreak, I'll share with you 12 steps to break out of your heartbreak, release your former relationship and move on.

Although I've walked these 12 steps, to put them into concepts and words, I needed the help of spiritual masters, teachers and authors. These concepts stem from spiritual teachings and age-old wisdom to help you move through your pain and heartbreak.

Each chapter focuses on a step in letting go.

Letting go is sacred because once you let go of heart pain and struggle, you have freedom of the heart, soul and spirit. You can break free of the familiarity of the past and accept the beauty and miracle of the unknown future.

You will go from a place of darkness to light.

It's very similar to the nature of enlightenment.

You continue to struggle and search until you find your true nature.

Letting go of heartbreak is like letting go of the ego, mind chatter, limiting beliefs and emotional turbulence we face as humans.

Letting go of heartbreak will help you awaken to who you are and find your spiritual nature – your inner essence or the real you.

You will burn in the fire but come out glowing.

We are about to embark on a sacred journey.

Join me at whatever step you're on today.

Blessings, friend,

Vishnu

1. The Step of Acceptance

"*To be in alignment with what is means to be in a relationship of inner nonresistance with what happens. It means not to label it mentally as good or bad, but to let it be.*" Eckhart Tolle, *A New Earth*

Where do journeys of love start?

Airports.

And before that, the internet, of course!

As I sat in that airport 18 years ago, I didn't know that my great love journey was about to begin.

Just 3 months earlier, I (a college student) and she (a doctor-to-be) had connected on the internet. We had found each other on a community directory from our shared community.

It was traditional in some sense because we had found each other in an Indian community that our parents would have expected us to remain and marry within.

It was unconventional because we had met each other on our own.

I had never dated or been in a relationship, as I knew in the back of my mind that a traditional, introduced, semi-arranged marriage was in my future. Not that my parents would introduce me to someone they would then force me to marry; instead, they would make the initial introductions and allow me to decide. Her family had similar expectations.

Yet, our internet connection, emails, Skype calls and chats quickly inspired me to purchase a ticket and make my way from San Diego (where I was studying) to India. A lifetime of cultural brain-washing, family expectations and guilty consciences flew out the door as I prepared to fly into the arms of a waiting lover.

My first trip began a 2-year romance that included many more trips, dramatic family objections and several challenges that distance created for us.

The family objections were as silly as the fact that our parents hadn't found each of us for the other person. They had not participated in the process and, thus, they didn't approve of our relationship. Both sets of parents were so similar, they each protested our relationship for the exact same reason.

It's hard to know today if they were against the relationship because they had not been part of the selection process or because perhaps they didn't believe we were right for each other and they opposed the relationship simply because they didn't see the compatibility we shared.

On top of our families' reservations and observations, the distance made our relationship difficult. Not being able to communicate easily – with technological limitations, time zones and her living with her parents – made communication, resolving problems and maintaining our relationship a challenge.

Little fights became big ones. Minor misunderstandings grew in severity. Grudges played out for days simply because we didn't have a chance to connect with one another.

While our relationship was on the rocks because of our parents' disapproval and because of our distance, we both believed it was simply the distance, time zones and lack of technological tools that were the problems. We thought that being together in the same country and in the same time zone would ease our relationship struggles and lead to a happily-ever-after life.

Somehow, we persevered and made it to our 2002 nuptials with the support of both our families. Yes, they had come around because they both saw the value of the other family; they came to appreciate how we had selected such good partners by ourselves. Or maybe it was because they had no choice and had to resign themselves to the fact that we were both stubborn and intent on getting married to each other!

We had imagined that our new lives together would be different than the rocky start we had experienced while being in different parts of the world and in different time zones. We looked forward to being together and starting a new life. We looked forward to harmony and compatibility, joy and the happily-ever-after we both desired.

Yet, expectations didn't match our hopes and desires.

The reality of living together became a wake-up call for both of us.

We communicated differently.

We fought differently.

We saw the world differently.

We valued different things and wanted different things out of life.

Our years together were challenging. Having grown up in different countries, and having different personalities and interests, we were at odds with each other over many things. Our introverted/extroverted personalities also created conflicts.

Unfortunately, the one thing we had in common was the thing that caused us the most grief and heartache. In each of our homes, we hadn't received the proper tools for relationships. As sensitive children, we found that the disciplined and strict manner in which our parents raised us had harmed our spirits. Our inability to communicate or express love crippled our own relationship.

We had not learned about the tools of love and consideration, give and take and compromise.

Our dominant fathers had a great influence over both of our lives; their demanding personalities took shape in both of us. Instead of compromise, we held firm in our positions. Instead of give and take, we demanded. Instead of respect and friendship, we found ourselves embroiled in fights, hurting each other unconsciously.

The fights were about small things and big things. The small things included how we spent our time, where we went on vacation and even where we went for dinner. The big things covered almost all the major differences a couple could have: money, career, housing, intimacy and the future.

With so many differences, I'm not sure how we remained together for as long as we did.

When we finally decided to pull the plug on the relationship, I wasn't prepared or willing.

In retrospect, it seems like a no-brainer. We were probably holding onto something that was dysfunctional and broken for much longer than necessary. Yet, at the time, it seemed like staying together was the right thing to do for the sake of our families, for the sake of certainty and for the sake of the possibility that things would improve in the future.

We initially took a 6-month break to determine whether we could get back together. When we returned, I proposed another attempt at salvaging our relationship. She proposed moving on with our lives separately and filing for divorce.

I reluctantly went along, hoping against hope that something would change. I was probably the more idealistic and sentimental of us, and I desired to keep our marriage intact. I was also probably the person who couldn't face the idea of breaking up, both for myself and for our families.

When you have 1,000 people at your wedding, including every closest member of your family, you feel obligated to stay married, at least for their sake. A separation and divorce mean you aren't just failing yourself, but all the people who love you most.

Regardless of my feelings about divorce, it seemed like the situation was out of my hands. I went along with it because she wanted it. Also, having practiced divorce law, I found the paperwork and legal aspects of getting a divorce to be pretty straightforward.

I never imagined that I would use my legal know-how and divorce law experience for myself.

For the longest time, I couldn't accept that the divorce was happening. However, like all universally designed things, the divorce was the quickest one I had ever done. The paperwork was flawless and the process ended after a mere 6 weeks.

The fallout would last for months and years.

For the first couple years after the divorce, I cried myself to sleep every night and wished that I would hear from my ex. I wanted to get back with her and I felt like I was stuck in a bad dream. Only positive and sentimental memories crept into my dreams every night.

Every day, I felt like this temporary separation would be over and we would be getting back together soon.

I couldn't come to terms with the fact that the relationship was over. I have since traveled the difficult journey from resistance to acceptance.

I've realized that to move on from something, you must be willing to accept it. This means allowing whatever happens to happen. You can change some circumstances in life but not others, even after you've done everything. Then it becomes a matter of confronting it, working through it and learning how to accept it.

To accept unimaginable circumstances and situations you can't do anything about, you must start by allowing it to be. You must look at a situation as neutral, not charged with strong emotions and beliefs. This may take some time.

To view a situation as neutral is to almost take the situation out of your mind and put it in front of you, like an object or a physical thing. It's to see a situation for what it is, not as your life ending or the end of all your hopes and dreams. If you are getting a divorce, you see it as two people separating their lives and going on to live new ones. If you have broken up, you see it as two people who have ended a relationship together and who are now living separately.

You add so much mind chatter and drama to situations. You look at relationships as life and death. You see relationships as black and white, in the most extreme circumstances. You – and I, to be fair – add all kinds of unnecessary and highly charged meanings to the circumstances of our lives.

What if you learned to see circumstances as they simply are? It's not good or not bad. It just is.

Acceptance doesn't take much energy. You're not doing anything. You're not changing anything, calling anyone, emailing anyone, flying across the country, speaking to his family, convincing your ex.

It's letting go and accepting the situation as it is. It's not doing anything to change the situation. It's fully immersing yourself in the situation at hand. Only when you fully accept a situation can you begin the process of moving on. Only when you breathe out completely and let go can you take in a new breath.

Acceptance becomes easier if you believe that everything is like nature, which means everything is perfect.

A flower blooms today, a tree dies tomorrow, a hurricane comes the next day. Nature evolves and happens without any of us doing anything. A wave can come in today and recede today. Today it might barely touch the shore and tomorrow it might flood the nearby town.

You don't like what nature does sometimes but do you always accept what it does? Don't you always talk about how to work around and through nature, or repair things after a natural disaster? We are not sitting there hoping something shouldn't happen or regretting that something did.

It's nature. Similar to the nature around us, our human nature should guide you to accept circumstances. Nothing is good or bad. Realize that everything is what it is; this is the first step to letting go.

For me, it took some time to get to the point of acceptance. It took me a couple of years to get over the fact that the divorce even happened. I had to let go of those notions of getting back together or replaying in my mind the highlights of our married life. I refused to let go of the relationship we had because it was comfortable and I knew it well.

I didn't think of divorce as simply two people ending a legally binding contract and moving on with their lives to be by themselves. I thought of divorce as the end of a generation of traditions. I thought of divorce as personal failure and shame to my family and community. I thought of divorce as the end of my personal well-being, my future and any hope for a normal life.

Now I can see how altered and skewed my thinking was but at the time, I was convinced that there was no point in living. My marriage was all I knew and my ex gave me my identity in many aspects of my life.

How could I possibly accept what I felt for a long time was unacceptable?

Well, I started viewing things in neutral terms. I had to change my mindset. I stopped believing all these dramatic and sentimental thoughts that were going through my mind. I began to distance myself from my thoughts, beliefs and feelings about the divorce. I had to look at this mind chatter more objectively rather than believe them hook, line and sinker.

Also, I began looking at this whole divorce as a natural occurrence rather than as some evil plot or bad karma. I looked at it like nature happening. You can't focus on the wreckage after a tsunami hits. When some bad natural event devastates a country, the residents don't lament for ages about the injustice or unfairness. People start picking up the pieces and rebuilding.

Accepting a circumstance and fully embracing it allows you improve those very circumstances. Hope, like a seed, grows out of the rubble and wreckage.

Only when you accept what happened can you fully deal with it.

When you see circumstances as they are, you will have more clarity about what to do next.

When you realize you can't change something, you begin to see what you can change.

Acceptance is fundamental to the moving-on process. If you can't soak in what happened, how can you heal from it, grow from it and rise from it?

The first step toward moving on is to accept what is. Accept it like nature minus your opinions, judgments and dramatic mind chatter.

Welcome it into your life without seeing it as good or bad. You never know what's good or bad. If you recall, some of the worst events of your life led to some of the best. And the best parts of your life led to disaster.

Accept what you cannot change because in the acceptance, your perspective, views and horizon will change.

2. The Step of Release

"When working with pain, give it space, allow it to be, and know that your awareness of the pain is separate from the pain itself. Opening to the pain allows it to be part of the reality you are witnessing and decreases the resistance to it, allowing you to relax around it. Open to what it is, acknowledge it, give it space, bring your awareness to it as another sensation. Pain is, and you are." Ram Dass, *Polishing the Mirror*

For much of my marriage, I was shut up and closed up.

Feelings would try to wash over me but I knew that wasn't a good thing. If you felt your feelings, I figured, you could get hurt. So I kept my feelings out of my marriage.

Can you imagine someone doing this?

Well, you could if you can understand that no one really taught me, or teaches anyone else, to process feelings.

School doesn't offer classes on emotions or feelings. You don't learn how to welcome, accept and transform the hard feelings that arise in your life.

Instead, society does one of three things with feelings. People deny that feelings exist. People use alcohol or drugs to reduce the pain of the feelings. Or people try to distract themselves so they don't have to confront the feelings that are arising.

Feelings are not a bad thing. Let me repeat: Feelings are not a bad thing. Even bad feelings are not bad.

This was a wakeup call to me because I had lived a good portion of my life disconnected from my feelings. I tried to deny, hide and cut myself off from my feelings.

Even during my marriage, feelings would wash over me but I would not allow myself to go there and feel them.

Strangely, I thought, based on what I had seen in my patriarchal and male-dominated family, that being the tough guy was the way to be a guy. So, yes, you felt a pang of feelings but as a strong man, you hid it. You didn't show it, you didn't discover it and you didn't talk about it!

Brené Brown, an author on the subject of vulnerability, would have had a fit if I had described to her my approach towards living in the world.

Fortunately, what happened is that when the divorce hit, I could not hold it all in.

Imagine I was a little shack filled with thousands of chicken eggs containing feelings. When the storm broke down the door, the eggs burst out into one large frying pan of scrambled eggs.

Terrible metaphor but my point is, my feelings spilled out at an uncontrollable speed.

I had no idea how to control them, manage them or deal with them.

I cried harder, longer and more deeply than I ever had in my life. Some days I had 4 or 5 crying episodes or more because of the sadness and loneliness. I'd never been used to crying like. Watching the tears flow as the memories flashed before me was pathetic but also helpful and useful.

I couldn't control it so I just allowed the feelings to come out. I did so without judging myself.

You must give your pain a seat at the table. Healing your pain starts with acknowledging your pain.

It starts with giving yourself the ability and freedom to express your pain.

Ideally, you want to do this the healthy way.

I let the pain come into my life without judging or berating myself. You'll experience pain and suffering, so let it happen. Nothing is wrong with you for feeling strong feelings. Nothing is wrong with uncomfortable emotions.

You could go wrong in how you care for these feelings after you've experienced them. Many people try to find a way, any way, to stop them or cut them off. Instead of alcohol, sex, drugs or a rebound relationship, let me suggest some healthier ways I dealt with my feelings.

I spoke to a couple of people about what I was going through. I wish I had done a lot more communicating. Feelings are heavy when you hold onto them yourself. When you're experiencing feelings on your own, you feel their burden and weight.

Women are much better at this than men are. They've done this their entire lives. Still, I've noticed even some women are reluctant to share their feelings.

I did it with a couple friends but more than that, I started sharing my feelings with a professional counselor.

Your feelings are not yours to bear alone, as you may believe. You don't have to feel embarrassed, weak or ashamed about your feelings. You can set down the heavy load of your feelings by talking to a professional, a therapist, a coach, a colleague or a friend. Share with the people you trust and who are close to you.

To share your feelings, you don't have to write a blog, either, but you can start writing them down to help you process them.

In my case, you're reading this book and Vishnu's Virtues, my blog, because I took it to an entirely different level – one that "normal" people usually don't. Not only did I want to share my feelings with a professional, I wanted to share my feelings with the world. I didn't want to keep a journal just for myself because I thought it wouldn't be meaningful enough.

As someone who looks for meaning in everything he does, I thought sharing with others would not only help me but also give hope to others on the same path. I found that my writing resonated with many people going through the same emotional experiences I was going through.

I spoke about it, I wrote about it and I prayed about it.

I've gone through quite a bit of spiritual growth and change since my divorce. Spirituality was another place that allowed me to sit with my feelings, present them to a higher being and find solace in the spiritual world. Sharing your feelings with a greater spirit or the universe causes those feelings to lose their impact or weight.

Feelings are not dirty and they are not a weakness. You should honor and embrace them. Feelings are the currency of life; you don't have to run from them. If they become overwhelming, get professional assistance. If not, learn to sit with them, experience them and share them with others.

When you continually feel your feelings, their weight and impact decreases. For example, when you burn your hand on the stove, it may hurt like the dickens on the first day. But with ointment and each passing day, the pain subsides.

It's the same with feelings. On day 1, they may be so overwhelming, you can't get through the day. They may be so painful, you'd rather not live and experience them. However, I've found that this perception tempers with each passing day.

Once you give yourself the pain and space to put your feelings out there, the Ram Dass quote at the top of this chapter comes into play. Over time and with practice, you see that you and the pain are not one and the same. There is you and there is pain. You are not pain. You experience pain and the pain you experience can lessen over time.

Pain resides in the feelings flowing through your body. However, become an observer of this pain and you'll notice it is just one of the many sensations within you.

The more mindful you become, and the more you notice the pain, the less it influences your life. The less grip it has on your life. Your identity does not become pain. Pain is just one of the experiences you encounter.

Instead of allowing pain to consume you, in her book *When Things Fall Apart*, Pema Chodron encourages you to explore and become curios about the pain.

"When we become inquisitive about these things, look into them, see who we are and what we do, with the curiosity of a young child, what might seem like a problem becomes a source of wisdom."

I mentioned spiritual practices like prayer; meditation is another way to sit with the pain. Any time you create quiet time and allow yourself to go within, and allow your feelings to unfold, you're becoming a pain whisperer and pain releaser.

When you meditate and focus on your breath, for example, you begin seeing that you're not pain but that pain is just one of the many feelings occupying your body. Giving yourself space to be silent gives you time to observe and sit with the pain. It gives you time to see that you and pain are separate. It reminds you that pain can enter your life and, yes, it can exit your life too.

Walking in nature, a stroll on the beach or other moments of reflection and mindfulness in your life can help you experience and burn away the pain you're experiencing.

Face the pain to simmer it. When you simmer the pain, you release it. When you release the pain, you continue your journey towards healing and letting go.

3. The Step of Melting Anger

"We can turn any part of our lives into a sacrifice, into an offering…If you're having trouble with someone, make them your practice. Add a picture of her or him to your altar. I take the people I'm having a real fierce time with, and I stick them on the puja table…Whatever else you do with another human being, never put them out of your heart." Ram Dass, *Paths to God*

A fundamental step towards moving on is burning the anger within.

You can be angry as long as you chose to be. I chose anger for a long time. It kept me from moving on.

I wasn't angry with my ex so much as I was angry with others, the circumstances and even myself.

After my divorce, I became an anger-fueled person. I was angry at my parents who had insisted we stay married and not get a divorce. I was angry at her parents who I believed had created some of the tension in our marriage. I was angry at her friends who might have encouraged her to take the first steps towards divorce.

I was angry at the Gods who might have cursed my life and desired to see me suffer.

I was angry at my ex because she had chosen to give up on the relationship and to not stay the cause. I blamed her for some of the things that had happened and I blamed her for the fact that my entire world had flipped upside down.

Finally, I was angry at myself for all the pain I was causing myself and others. I was angry at myself for not being the kind of man I was capable of being. I was angry at myself for disappointing both our families. I was angry that I couldn't take the high road at times, that I couldn't avoid being argumentative and that, towards the end of my marriage, I was acting like a person I didn't even recognize anymore.

I was a ball of fiery anger which consumed and burned me. I chose this place for a long time and refused to make any changes.

What's the gift of anger, you ask? Being stuck in the past, being a ball of negative energy and treating yourself and others around you terribly.

You had a negative and horrific experience, and you continue this experience by allowing the anger to consume you and direct your life.

I learned that to reduce the fiery fumes of anger, I had to release the anger towards others and towards myself.

First, Ram Dass suggests treating other people as a practice and offering. He suggests treating people as altars where you work on releasing anger.

The practice of forgiving others starts with a choice. You must choose forgiveness and move towards forgiveness every chance you get.

This isn't easy because usually you will choose not to forgive. You want other people to feel the pain and suffering you felt over what they did to you. You want others to suffer the same way you did, so you hold your forgiveness. Or you say to yourself that you'll forgive when you are ready.

One, you'll never get to a place of being ready. Two, the quicker you forgive, the quicker you move. What they say is true; you forgive for yourself, not for other people. It's actually counter-intuitive.

At times in your life, people burn you and hurt you. The best way to get back at them, we wrongly surmise, is to be angry and hold a grudge. Actually, the best way to get back at people is to forgive them and let them go from your life. If you hold onto your anger and pain, you'll suffer more and remain in pain longer. You'll keep those people in your life longer.

As much as you think it to be true, you're not hurting them with your anger. You're not hurting them with your lack of forgiveness, with your resentment and by not speaking to them. They have no idea what you're angry about…or that you're so angry in the first place!

You're simply hurting yourself, so why not release yourself from them by forgiving them?

Forgive even when you're not ready. Forgive continuously because sometimes you're not ready but you still set an intention to forgive them. You may have to do this over the course of many days or months. Sometimes what people did to you is so bad, you can't bring yourself to forgive them but you can take smaller steps.

Some days, you can simply say that you're setting an intention to forgive them. One day, you can write (for your eyes only) a list of reasons to forgive them. Every day you can proclaim words of forgiveness to the trespasser even if you're not there and aren't ready yet.

Get into the habit of practicing forgiveness to let go a little more each day.

Forgiveness is the key to moving on from the past.

If you really want to get back at someone or do something to make the person who hurt you angry, forgive them. Release the control that other people have over you.

One way to melt the hurt and anger so you can forgive is to look at the other person's positive qualities or any redeeming value they might have.

Look at any positive thing they have done or any way they made your life better after the pain they caused.

Try to create a list of positive reasons why the person did what they did.

Forgive them for the sake of karma. If you forgive someone you really didn't want to forgive, one day you'll receive the benefits of someone forgiving you.

Forgive them for spiritual reasons. You and the culprit are cut from the same cloth. You and the person who caused the pain are one and the same. To forgive them is to forgive yourself. You are part of the same universal spirit that the other person is cut from; you and the pain-causer are one and the same.

To let go of the anger towards yourself, you must remind yourself that you're only human and you're doing the best you can do. Remind yourself that you had certain skills, a certain upbringing and certain characteristics for handling life, and you used those things to the best of your ability.

If you blame yourself or hold yourself responsible, look at all those circumstances that were out of your control. Look at all the things you are not directly responsible for that would have occurred with or without you.

Instead of burning with anger, burn with something else. Burn with love, compassion, empathy and understanding towards yourself. Cultivate love and affection within yourself so you can give yourself a break.

To further melt anger, observe it every time it arises within you. Remind yourself that you can better handle your life's problems and circumstances if you have anger under control.

When you're angry, you lose all sense of control and ability. You allow anger to run your life.

If you want to make better decisions and come from a place of rational and intelligent thought, you must get a hold of fiery anger in your life. Observe anger, welcome anger, sit with and allow anger to burn within. The more you watch anger, the quicker you will melt its intensity in your life.

Once you're aware of this guest who rages in your house, you will become more conscious of whenever it shows up. You'll be able to address it and work on melting the anger sooner once you see it.

Acknowledgment and awareness is the first step to putting out the fire of anger.

The quicker the anger melts towards others and yourself, the quicker you'll move on.

You learn to tame anger so it works for you, not against you.

Use the fire extinguisher within (spiritual practices and emotional healing) to water down the anger.

Time can usually temper anger. If you get angry very quickly, get into the practice of noticing when the anger arrives. Then breathe into the anger for a few breaths. Or take a brief timeout so your anger can cool down. Leave the place you're in, walk around the house or undertake any kind of physical activity to buy yourself time and allow the anger to taper off.

If necessary, speak to professionals in the mental health field to help you cope with raging anger.

Listen to sermons from wise men, preachers and mentors.

Strive to live the virtues of every religion which instructs you on taming anger.

Befriend anger and allow it to guide you, teach you, instruct you and help you make better decisions.

Don't allow it to hold you captive and keep you in a personal prison of the past.

4. The Step of Choice

"When we can recognize that we have a habit of replaying old events and reacting to new events as if they were old ones, we can begin to notice when that habit energy comes up. We can then gently remind ourselves that we have another choice." Thich Nhat Hanh, *Fear: Essential Wisdom for Getting Through the Storm*

You may not believe you can move on.

This is fatalistic thinking that kept me stuck for years.

You believe that because life crushed you and your heart broke, you don't have much control over life.

When my breakup started brewing and the divorce happened, I tried to stop it. I tried to figure out ways to stay in the marriage and not split up. Yet despite my many actions, the divorce proceeded.

So, I got caught up in this idea that I had no control over any aspect of my life. I began believing I was powerless; a leaf tossed around in this tornado of life. No matter what I did, life would end up the same way for me. It would always be painful.

I then began taking comfort in the past and the high points of the marriage. I would reminisce, reflect upon and have sentimental thoughts about what had happened. I would replay all the wonderful times we had, all her positive qualities and all the special moments we shared.

As a coping mechanism, I habitually repeated past positive experiences in my mind. I dreamed and daydreamed about all the good times of the past because this was a source of comfort. It was like having a favorite blanket or photo album that brought back good feelings.

Continuously going to the past and marinating there was a good coping mechanism but it kept me stuck in the past. For years, it prevented me from moving on. I was a prisoner who enjoyed remaining stuck in a place I knew well. See, healing and moving on were novel, uncertain concepts. I didn't know what would happen in the future, which was scary, but I knew what had happened in the past and that was comforting.

I've come to discover that we as humans despise the uncertain and unknown.

We will do whatever it takes to maintain the status quo. We will do whatever it takes to remain in a place we know. That's why we stay in bad relationships and marriages, right? You'd rather be in something terrible and known than in something new and novel.

During this time in my life, I remained stuck in two places. One, I believed life was life and I had very little control over how it unfolded. Two, I believed the past was better than the present so I continued living in that place. I continued reflecting on and staying in my happy thoughts of the good things that had happened in the past.

Over the years, I realized both things were, in fact, harming me and holding me back.

I realized my most powerful weapon, which I had suppressed out of fear, and which you have too, is the power of choice.

Choice is the weapon you need to move on.

You can't change much of what will happen to you, regardless of your preferences or desires.

The good, the bad and the ugly all unfold, regardless of how you feel about those circumstances.

You're on a sailboat and you have no control over the windstorms that arrive to topple you but you do have control over something. You have control over what you'll do after the windstorm hits. You have control over rebuilding and starting over. You have control over how you deal with the circumstances in front of you.

You have the choice of starting to grieve the past and work through the hurt so you can move on with your life.

You have the choice of forgiving others and letting go of the anger towards the people who hurt you.

You have the choice of getting out of bed and making the best of your day, every day.

You have the choice of dating and meeting people again.

You have the choice of releasing yourself from the past, of stopping it from playing over and over in your mind.

You may not have the power of circumstance but you do have the power of choice.

No matter how bad or gloomy your life is, there's always a silver lining, a sliver of hope or a positive outcome that's available for you. Your only job is to not give up and to find that silver lining.

I'm going to share with you how to use the power of choice to stop living in the past and to navigate the next chapter of your life.

You have a choice to live in a sad yesterday or an uncertain tomorrow but the middle ground is this moment in front of you. Later on, an entire chapter is devoted to living in the moment but for now, just know that living in the moment is a choice.

When you're dreaming of the past or seeing yourself fearing the future, watch your mind and bring yourself back to the current moment.

Remind yourself that you have no control over the past and you don't have to let it rule the rest of your life.

Although you're certain about the past, remember that your life can start over only when you let go of the past and embrace the uncertainty of today.

At the moment, you don't have to live for the future but for right now.

In this moment, you're content, happy, free.

This very moment you're reading this book, you're completely fine. There is no pain, struggle, tears or heartbreak right now.

Only when you think about your life in whole or dwell on these hurtful moments do you remain stuck. However, remind yourself that you're choosing this.

You don't have to live in this place that no longer exists.

Your wanting to remain in the past is a decision of comfort and an intentional choice.

You have the willpower, ability and conscious thought to live in this moment.

To start this process of choice, catch yourself drifting off into the past. See how many of your waking and sleeping hours you spend reminiscing on all the good times with your ex. Observe your tendency to live in the past.

Once you become aware of what you're doing, you have more knowledge and ability to bring yourself forward to today.

Keep catching yourself as you drift into the past and observe how long you spend soaking your mind and dreams there.

Once you get sick of being there and as you begin to wake up to the realization that you don't have to live there, you'll start taking more conscious actions to be present today.

Again, later chapters will talk more about how to bring yourself to the present moment but for now, the most critical way to be present is to choose to be present. Yes, that power is in your hands and your mind.

You don't have to be in the prison of your past. You have the choice to insert the key in the jail cell of the past and walk out of it. The key is in your pocket and is always available to you whenever you're ready to walk out towards freedom.

Only when you get sick of living in this non-existent land of the past can you start living in the land of today.

In addition to the choice of not living in the past, you have many choices you may not realize about today and your future.

You may feel your circumstances are limited and your future hopeless but you don't realize how much power you have in your hands.

In any situation that feels hopeless or dark, you must ask yourself what it is you can do despite all the many things you can't do.

What power do you have?

What do you want out of life?

You have the ability to ask these questions at any point and to open up your life to possibilities.

See, when you go through brutal breakups, you awaken to the emotional reality of what you are facing. You awaken to the problems, the hurts and the pain, and so you remain stuck there. I challenge you to try something different.

I ask you to explore or entertain the idea of what you actually want in relationships and life.

Once you see a brighter and more positive picture, one that sadness and pain doesn't hold down, you'll begin to see the possibilities. You'll begin to see that you have choices you can actually do something about. You'll begin to see that you have different decisions you can make.

One exercise to complete here is to regularly visualize what you want. Put yourself in a place and envision the life you want to see around you. Feel the place, breathe the place and take comfort in this new place you can create.

Once you begin to see what's possible, you'll begin to see that you don't have to stay stuck in the same old place of the past.

Once you can dream about new relationships and opportunities in your future life, you'll become more excited about your life and future.

The idea isn't to focus on problems and where you've been; it's to focus on solutions and what's possible for you.

Another positive way to approach life when you're feeling stuck in the past is to remind yourself of every other dilemma or life obstacle you've faced. You've always found a way out, right?

Reflect on other parts of your life and other moments in your life when you felt stuck. You somehow always found a way to overcome it and move on. Why not do the same now?

You certainly know what it's going to take for you to move on.

What will it take? Get a sheet of paper and fill up one side with as many solutions as you can think of to help people move on from heartbreak. Just write down ideas like you're giving advice to another person.

After you flip the page, reflect on what you've just written and what solutions can you implement in your own life.

For example;

"I'm going to get out of the house once a week and start attending group classes so I meet more people."

"I'm going to stop feeling alone by reaching out to a new friend every day."

"I'm going to get more active in the community and start doing some volunteer work."

"I'm going to call a counselor and see if I can make an appointment to help myself let go of this broken relationship once and for all."

"I'm going to find a coach to help me figure out what I want out of life."

As you do this, and as you choose the strategies that will work for you, you'll realize that, yes, you do have choices. Determining which strategies to pursue is a testament to the power of your choice.

Finally, motivation to make choices comes from the fact that other relationships have positive outcomes.

Instead of talking to friends who have gone through breakups and divorces, expand your circle to include people in successful relationships. You – and I at one time – found this hard to believe, but they are out there.

When you're going through heartbreak, the universe kindly introduces you to people going through similar or worse situations and you feel a spirit of camaraderie. After a while, though, this can get old and cumbersome. You'll feel sad and frustrated, as though a successful relationship will never happen for you.

To change the realm of possibilities, hang out with people who are in good relationships.

Look for people in committed, long-term and happy relationships.

Don't use your life or the life of your broken-hearted circle as the measuring rod. Give yourself opportunities to see positive and encouraging relationships.

Keep reminding yourself that you can have the opposite experience of what you've been through.

The past doesn't have to repeat itself; you can have as good of a relationship as the best couples you know.

Choices. Choices. Choices.

Life can throw its heartiest and toughest punches at you but you can catch those punches, melt those punches, turn those punches around and punch life back.

All you have to do is make a new choice and a new decision.

Yes, life can do its part and you may have little control over that fact but you can react to life's ups and downs in your own way.

You can choose a new partner, a new life and a new future. You can choose a new reaction, a new perspective and new actions.

You have the power to change yourself and your circumstances; you can do this through your perspective and the way you view things. You have this formidable superpower called choice.

5. The Step of Learning

"When we review the past and observe it deeply, if we are standing firmly in the present, we are not overwhelmed by it…We can learn from them…That is called 'looking at something old in order to learn something new.'" Thic Nhat Hanh, *Essential Writings*

In my marriage, I learned what I didn't like about my spouse and what didn't work in our relationship.

I kept a detailed account of her personality and how its difficult parts made our marriage hard.

I also noticed that all the things we didn't do (compromise, negotiate, give in, treat each other respectfully, communicate with each other) were what led to our divorce.

For the longest time since the end of the marriage, and even during our marriage, I had strongly believed that my ex was much to blame for many of our issues. Her upbringing, childhood and personality traits made her the person she was. Her many issues led to the conflict in our relationship.

I was convinced that all our problems stemmed from her and I placed most of the blame for our divorce on her. Now, years later, I've come to realize that, in fact, the opposite was true.

She may have had some issues but regardless of them, she awakened the many issues inside me.

Why does this realization matter?

Well, as you're reflecting on your past relationship, you may have considered what worked and what didn't. You may have blamed all kinds of places and people outside yourself.

While I'm not saying you're completely at fault for your relationship troubles, I am suggesting that your ex likely brought forward many issues you now must examine.

Your ex, like it or not, was your greatest spiritual and life teacher. This means your job is to understand the lessons you can learn from that former relationship and become more self-aware.

Your job isn't to nitpick your ex or to be upset about the lessons they taught you or the issues they triggered in you.

Staying upset with your ex and all the trouble they caused you is unproductive. Most importantly for our purposes here, it will keep you stuck in the past.

The way to transform the bitterness, anger and frustration you experienced with your ex into something valuable to you is to see your ex as a teacher and to see the pain they caused you as a lesson.

Again, how you view it is your choice, but seeing your ex as a pain-causer and heartbreaker will just keep you fuming about the past and unable to do anything to correct the situation.

Instead, if you consider the person to be a lesson, you can use your ex as a study. You can pick up invaluable lessons to improve your own life and, best of all, avoid these types of people and characteristics in the future.

In your dating life, you'll have a better idea of what kind of partners to look for. In your personal life, you'll be more adept at handling difficult personalities. In your professional life, you can spot and manage the kinds of characters who are similar to your ex.

You observe the specific behaviors and characteristics that hurt you or pushed your buttons. You then use your awareness to get better at relationships and better manage those irritations you experience. You can use your learnings from your ex to show up as a better partner the next time around.

The fact that you change partners doesn't make the trigger points go away.

Your ex brought up under-the-surface issues that are bothering you but that you could never have noticed on your own. Our partners can trigger our wounds, pains and emotional hurts. You may despise your ex for doing this unless you see this as your opportunity to work on your inner thorns.

Your partners can raise issues within you that you now must notice. These dormant issues are for you to uncover, discover and work on.

In my case, I took words and criticism from my ex especially hard. Her words were particularly sensitive to me due to my upbringing, so they brought out the worst in me. I would then respond similarly with increasing hostility and vileness.

Our words became a nuclear attack on each other; we both pounced on each other's self-worth, abilities, characteristics, successes, etc. until we had torn down each other completely.

During our marriage, I thought what she did was unfair and was due to her upbringing. I didn't focus on anything within myself. However, with time after the divorce, I began to notice that the harsh words we had used against each other had to do with my sense of self-worth, my self-esteem and how I felt about myself.

Our fights uncovered unresolved anger at my parents and other people in my life. They touched on my brewing self-hatred. Words had the same impact on me as the physical lashings I had received as a child.

For her, too, words were verbal bombs. We launched these bombs freely to destroy each other.

So much was going on underneath our fights that we both hardly had time to notice it. We were preoccupied with tearing at each other and bringing each other down.

It took time and distance from this relationship for me to realize that the things she triggered within me were hardly about her and all about me. They had to do with my childhood, upbringing and emotional wounds.

The way to take concrete lessons from your ex is to reflect upon and write down the common fights and disagreements that existed between you and your ex. Also, note the character traits in your ex that really irritated you or brought out the worst in you.

You likely never consciously reflected on what happened in your relationship or what your fights were about. Now is your time to become more observant and aware of what happened.

In these observations, instead of focusing on what your ex did and how they hurt you, become more observant of what they triggered in you. What behaviors, emotional wounds and inner thorns did they strike?

With the passing of time and reflection on these questions, you will have more clarity about what you must do next.

First, ask yourself what version of yourself you'd like to be instead of someone who allows these characteristics to limit them.

How will you commit to changing these things about yourself?

How will you work on these inner faults and shortcomings? Therapy, counseling, coaching, new habits, mindfulness or …?

Make the necessary changes and improvements to these faulty areas in your life. Use new relationships as continued practice for improving and developing these character traits that are holding you back as a person.

As you start working on these inner thorns and as you continue dating more people, you'll know who more deeply touches these inner thorns and whom you are more compatible with.

Although you're working on your inner self, also be aware of whom you're attracting into your life and who is better for you.

This is another way you're learning about yourself. You're getting to know who pushes your buttons and who simply touches your buttons.

Whom can you get along with more, work with more, love more? Make these assessments as you're dating so you're learning about yourself and growing as a person.

Based on past mistakes and decisions, make wiser decisions. Don't repeat your mistakes and continually find the same type of partners.

Some people will push buttons while others will make you aware of these inner trigger buttons in a loving but awakening way. They will support you in healing these inner triggers. Look for these kinds of partners – the ones who not only push the buttons but pull you along towards waking up.

Look for the trigger points and sources of conflict so you're not attracting the same type of person over and over again.

Yes, you're working on yourself but some partners can make you work on yourself so much that you get closer to reaching spiritual enlightenment!

If you're not seeking immediate spiritual enlightenment, get better at romance and date more wisely.

Look for partners who don't trigger your inner thorns as much.

Make better choices with the partners you find. End relationships quicker if you see patterns from previous partners. Learn from both your past and current relationships.

Move on quicker from relationships that end and move closer towards the right person.

Your exes can help you become a better person overall and a better person in relationships as well.

Learning which types of people and relationships don't work will help you get out of the vicious pattern of bad relationships and move towards the person who is meant for you.

Again, all of your exes can be your greatest teachers if you allow them to be.

Let relationships be your classroom. Let your exes be your teachers.

Look back and into your past relationships and become an observer of not what he/she did, but how it bothered you.

If you start looking at your past like you're a student rather than a perturbed lover, you'll be able to not only move on quicker but move on with valuable insights into and advice on becoming a better person.

With a student mentality, you can become a better partner, person and human being.

6. The Step of Connectedness

"If you are locked into the idea of a separate self, you have great fear. But if you look deeply and are capable of seeing 'you' everywhere, you lose that fear." Thich Nhat Hanh, *Fear: Essential Wisdom for Getting Through the Storm*

You get so caught up with your ex and you don't know what planet he or she came from.

You can't imagine two people more different than yourselves.

I was spiritual and introverted. She was more practical and extroverted.

I enjoyed staying home. She liked going out.

I was compassionate and understanding, I believed.

She was judgmental and condescending, I thought.

I came from a good family and she came from a dysfunctional one, my mind told me.

I represented goodness and she represented all the bad things in the world.

In the passionate hatred of each other, you can clearly see divisions. You can clearly see separation. You and the other person are two completely different people from different universes.

After the breakup, believing this separateness theory will keep you stuck longer.

When you think "him versus me" or "me versus her," your mind gets caught up in all the chaos and dysfunction of your relationship.

You think about how right you were and how wrong your ex was; what a good person you are and what an evil person your ex is.

When you think of your partner as the polar opposite of you, you create divisions in your mind. You polarize the person and take an extreme view of them. You see things as good and bad, black and white, positive and negative.

These thoughts create permanent divisions between you and also lead you to remain mentally and emotionally embroiled in your past relationship.

Such thoughts also allow your ego to rule the day and to cultivate more anger and resentment towards your ex.

They leave you with the bitter taste of the past and make you continue living in the past, allowing your mind to remain preoccupied with how bad your ex was.

Seeing your ex as separate isn't healthy for future relationships, either.

Instead of seeing partners as one unit who respect and love each other, you see future partners as potential enemies. You see division in the past, which makes you see division in the future.

If you're interested in moving on, you must do much of the forgiveness work we spoke about earlier. You must put the past to rest. Part of that involves seeing the oneness with your former partner.

Oneness means you and your ex are connected; you are both cut from the same cloth.

To see more connectedness and less separation between you and your ex, you must start seeing the universality of everything.

Everybody shares the sun, air, trees, sky and water.

We, as humans, are part of the greater fabric of the universe. However, simply because we look different, wear different clothes and are members of different social classes, we believe we are different from each other.

We begin to think that because we have different skin colors and speak different languages in different parts of the globe, we are inherently different.

Nothing can be further from the truth.

Your ego makes you believe you're separate and different.

Who you are is completely random and happenstance. You do the work you do and you are the person you are.

The same elements, biochemistry and atoms compose each person. We are nearly identical except for our outward appearances, social status and other characteristics of circumstance.

The point here may be a little on the spiritual side but essentially, we are all one and the same.

Even the ex who angered, upset and fought with you is the same as you are.

We are not in separate cups of water. We are all in one aquarium called earth. No matter which part of that aquarium you're in, the water that touches you in one area is the same water that awaits you in another area.

If you see the connectedness between you and your ex, and if you let go of the mental differences, you'll be able to move on quicker.

To be more connected, notice the spiritual nature of all people. Look at the elements and characteristics you share with the people around you. You don't have commonality with just your family but with your community and beyond as well.

Look at the inner nature and who the person is beneath their status, car and profession. Start noticing the common things about you and everyone around you.

Instead of looking at differences and judging folks, consciously look for the ways in which someone is similar to you. How is their story and background similar to yours? How are their inspirations and aspirations similar to yours? How are their problems and struggles similar to yours?

Can you start seeing yourself in other people's shoes? If someone is going through something difficult, can you imagine what it would be like to stand where they are? If someone tells you a story of hardship and struggle growing up, can you feel what it must be like to be them? Can you look at life from their perspective?

This doesn't have to be someone you know. Look for strangers, people you read about or watch on television. Put yourself in their shoes and look at the world from their perspective.

Another way to decrease separateness and increase connectivity is to be the kind of person you want others to be to you. Treat others and act towards them how you want them to respond to you.

Before you think about or judge someone, put yourself in the shoes of the person you're thinking about or judging.

Before you say or do something to someone, imagine what it would be like if they did that to you.

Whatever action you take towards someone, imagine that the other person takes that action towards you.

Live your life according to the golden rule. You will see not only a connection to your ex but a connection to everyone in your life.

Your task is to see everyone as one and part of you so you will not only move on from your past but fully embrace your future with connection, fulfillment and happiness with others.

Tear down the walls standing between you and love, between you and the present, between you and the life waiting for you.

Tear down the wall of separation and embrace the connection all around you.

7. The Step of This Moment

"We can learn not to keep situations or events alive in our minds, but to return our attention continuously to the pristine, timeless present moment rather than be caught up in mental movie-making." Eckhart Tolle, *A New Earth*

Living in this moment is a choice.

As I mentioned previously, when you get really sick of the past, you get to the point of wanting to live in this moment.

For some of us, this will take ages because, as I've mentioned before, the past is comfortable and certain.

You and I relish living there.

That's why we take so long to move on. That's why many people don't want to move on.

Who wants to leave a place of comfort, a place they have known their entire life?

The past is a soothing place where you know how things turned out. You don't have to face the unknown. You know the outcome. You don't have to suffer because you know how the past turned out. Even if it ended badly, you know the outcome, so you relish and take comfort in this place in the past.

It goes without saying that to move on with your life, you must be willing to leave the past in the past.

The first strategy to do this is simply awareness. Notice how much your mind tries to take you back to the past and how comforting you find it.

The more you notice yourself doing this, the more you'll get sick of it. You'll soon begin to see that you are losing what's happening today to what has already happened.

Not only has life hurt you in some way but it's now robbing you of living today.

You're experiencing loss not just once but with more intensity each day you think about it.

Once you notice this, you must actively choose to get present. You must consciously choose to not return to this happy place of certainty and knowingness. You must be willing to start living life today.

One technique to help with all this is being mindful of your thoughts. This is why mindfulness is becoming more popular today. Mindfulness is simply noticing what your mind is doing. Instead of allowing the monkey mind to entertain itself, we become more present about what it's actually doing.

Mindfulness is watching this mind and becoming an observer of it.

Meditation is a practice that can help you with this. Many types of meditation have you focus on a certain point, your breath or a mantra, or a light in your third eye. As you focus on one point and thoughts begin to arise, you can observe them and watch the mental gymnastics going on in front of you.

As you watch your thoughts pass by you in meditation, you'll become aware of what your mind is doing all the time.

Even when you're not meditating, get into a game of catching your mind taking you back to the past. Say out loud, "There it goes again." The more you observe and the more you notice your mind doing this, the better you'll get at stopping it from going to the past.

As you get into this practice of watching your mind, you'll come to see that you and your mind are not one.

You may think about everything frequently, but this doesn't mean you are your thoughts.

You're "you" and your thoughts are your thoughts.

You are becoming the observer of your thoughts. You are becoming the observer of the past.

As you get into this practice of separating yourself from the past, you'll begin to see how you're not your thoughts. You'll then see that you're not your past either. If your thoughts are your past and you're not your thoughts, you're not your past.

As you make this distinction, you'll realize that you can put away your thoughts and your past. You can stop replaying these thoughts which reside within your mind. Your thoughts are a temporary resident, not a permanent resident.

Another way to live in the present moment is to stop spending your time lying around in bed or lounging around at home, thinking only of the past.

You reflect and reminisce only when your mind is idle and you have nothing to do, so keep busy.

Fill your time with activities, sports, leisure and friends who help you live for today. The more you live for today and keep yourself preoccupied with activities that engage your mind, the less likely you are to slip away into the past.

However, not every activity helps. The activities that keep you most engaged in the moment are the best choices. Activities like dancing, running or other forms of physical exertion will keep you engaged in the moment. Participate in activities that require focus and concentration so that you won't have the energy or ability to go into your happy place in the past.

One last suggestion to live here in the moment is to be constantly aware of what's going well today. If you can note the good things in your life and acknowledge them on a daily basis, you will be able to appreciate the life in front of you.

Even if you don't have a partner today or aren't experiencing love now, your life contains other positive and happy circumstances. Be appreciative and actively acknowledge the people who make you smile, the comforts you enjoy and the good in your life.

8. The Step of Going Within

"If you can experience this silence, your mind begins to shift…If you remain on the path and keep experiencing inner silence, peace dawns, and then joy and bliss. This is the unfoldment of the true self. It's the whole meaning of 'going inside'." Deepak Chopra, *Spiritual Solutions*

Fights happen between two people.

Communication and counseling amongst a couple happen with a therapist.

Family and friends – at least in our case – got involved and became vocal champions for our marriage.

People I had never heard from called me with marriage tips and reasons to stay together.

Divorces happen in courtrooms full of lawyers and other judges.

So much of the relationship and your breakup is a public process. Many voices and people are involved, so when it comes to healing and reparation, you must go in the opposite direction.

During the healing process, you must drown out all the noise around you.

Without your ex in the picture, you will finally have the quiet time to process what has happened.

While it's good to have a circle of people to consult, talk to and get encouragement from, true healing comes from a little quiet time and silence.

This applies to you if you're an extroverted person and spend much of your time interacting with others. This also applies if you're an introverted person whose mind always contains many thoughts. You may be alone but your thoughts may also overly preoccupy you.

You want to go within so you can process, understand and know yourself better. It will help you figure out who you are beneath it all so you have more self-clarity and life clarity. Going within will help you figure out what's important to you and what doesn't matter in life.

It will also help you get past the mind chatter and reach your true inner being.

Learning to be by yourself, to know yourself and get in alignment with yourself will help you take the next steps forward.

With your ex, you might have even lost a sense of who you are.

Going within will help you get "ok" with being by yourself. If you were with a partner for a long time, you won't be comfortable being by yourself. You're so used to another person in your space, and you're so attached to this person, you may not be able to stand the silence and being alone.

Silence and going within will help you get to know yourself again and start over with more clarity.

Just to be clear (and I talk about this in later chapters), I'm suggesting that you carve out some downtime to go within and be by yourself, not that you become a recluse or hermit and burn in the pain and suffering of heartbreak! Don't shut yourself in your house, lock the doors and cry for 12 hours a day.

We are talking about some downtime – alone time that allows you to do the inner work necessary for awareness and growth.

For me, going within took many spiritual forms. I engaged in many types of activities that allowed me to get to know myself. This included traveling on my own to Central America and living by myself in Costa Rica and Nicaragua. While I stayed at hostels and farms, I had a lot of quiet time to reflect and ask myself life's deeper questions.

In Nicaragua, I spent time going to churches and listening to sermons as I tried to recover from my divorce. In these sacred spaces, I prayed and let the divine light fill my body and soul. I allowed myself to be alone with light coming in, offering clarity and healing.

Later, I traveled to India for much spiritual healing and cleansing. I traveled to many temples in South India, praying for the strength and courage to let go of what had happened in my life.

Per South Indian temple customs, there were Vedic rituals that included burning and fire as priests chanted powerful Vedic shlokas. There was a burning of food items in a ceremony called a homa. The burning of symbolic food items generates powerful divine vibrations. To me, the process is like burning what is no longer there so you can start over. The ashes, to me, represent a place where you can begin again.

Life circumstances can burn down the house. Our spiritual awakening also requires a burning. When external circumstances burn, you must burn down everything within.

Being in spiritual places gives you space and silence to burn it all down within. It gives you the time and space to reflect by yourself and commune with higher powers. It gives you the space to have an emotional cleansing and letting go. It allows you to take a breath to what was and bid it goodbye from your life.

You go within to close a chapter and release whatever is holding you back.

You go within by actively creating time for yourself and getting out of the hamster-wheel life you're living. It's taking trips and excursions that require planning and conscious effort to do things by yourself. The fewer people around you, the more time you can spend alone.

Create time to visit natural settings, sacred spaces and spiritual grounds.

Go to places with strong vibrations of a healing spirit. Physical places that are ripe for heart mending and soul awakening.

What are you supposed to do when you go within?

I've talked about many of the practices in this book.

Allow yourself to feel the feelings of the past, to grieve and let go.

Give yourself an opportunity to forgive your ex and other people who hurt you. You can do this by visualizing forgiveness. Continuously forgive all the people who hurt you.

Speak words of completion as you thank them for coming into your life. Thank them for the lessons they taught you and for sharing part of the life journey with you.

Let them know their task in your life is over. They've helped you get to where you are; they have given you the self-awareness you'll take with you.

From within, radiate forgiveness and then love to your ex and all those around you from your past.

Once you work on the letting-go part, go within to discover who you are.

Burn from within to release all the aspects of your identity, including your race, profession, social standing, etc.

Visualize yourself as the ash. Then ask yourself who you really are.

Who are you in spirit and soul?

Who is the essential you?

Who is this person when you take away personality, character and outward appearances?

Get to the bottom of you. Get to the light of you.

Discover this inner spark when you go within and connect to that place in your life.

Then go forward in life connected to this spark; living a life of meaning and purpose.

9. The Step of Soul Awakening

"Every experience that you encounter is the most appropriate experience that is possible for you to encounter at the moment that you encounter it. Every response that you choose creates consequences that you will experience." Gary Zukav, *Soul to Soul*

Prior to my divorce, I thought spirituality and religion were practices I did mechanically. These were rituals I participated in to get external things I wanted. I treated God and the higher powers as entities who helped me get what I wanted in life.

I meditated and prayed for my marriage to stay together so I wouldn't have any problems. I asked for financial stability, emotional maturity and a partner who would wise up.

Little did I realize that this isn't what spirituality is about. It's not about asking for stuff and demanding that life work out a certain way. It's not demanding that people behave a certain way.

As I talked about a little bit before, spirituality is getting to your truth, light and essence.

It's unpeeling who you are so you can start living from this place. So much of our existence consists of putting on masks, wearing titles and showing up a certain way in the world.

Spirituality is the opposite. It's the taking away. It's the disrobing of all your external qualities and looking at what's left.

Your ex can help you take away all the masks and reduce you to you.

Every painful experience you've had will help you take off the masks quicker, understand yourself better and live a truer version of yourself.

Similar to letting go of your past, in this process, you let go of the past "you's". You must shed the many layers of yourself so you can let go of your ex and your past. This requires letting go of who you were.

This process of letting go of your old self and becoming a newer version of yourself is exactly why you went through all the situations you did. Your trials and tribulations have helped mold you into who you are today.

The process has uncovered and stripped away your previous identities. To let go of the past is to let go of these former identities.

To help you unpeel the layers, ask yourself what your ex is here to teach you – not about themselves or about your ability to choose partners, but about what your ex awakened or triggered. Reflect on what personal, spiritual and emotional lessons you learned from this person.

Next, what was the reason for that entire experience? What did that relationship teach you?

In the larger context, this relationship existed to help you learn some things about your life, the world and your place in it.

What are the big life lessons you picked up from this experience with your ex?

In the future, what will you do more of or less of?

Now that all these unknown qualities, these trigger points and this lack of comfort are open in you, who have you become?

Determine whether you must do internal work.

For example, in my case, I realized I had much work to do about my anger, resentments and emotionally abusive behavior. Counselors helped me put a spotlight on these areas in my life. I literally asked professionals how I could resolve these issues.

I started working on these issues within myself – areas that not only affected my relationship with my ex-wife but likely existed in all aspects of my life.

You must start working on these issues because they will show up again in your next relationship.

Not only what happened in the past, but these moments of healing you're experiencing will raise issues that you will deal with in the present moment as you're trying to heal.

You may try to do everything I mention in this book and fail occasionally but it's not about succeeding or failing at letting go. It's being open to the process, learning and growing.

The wise Buddhist monk, Pema Chodron's spiritual practice is staying in the off-center, in-between state of life. This is the place she says in **When Things Fall Apart: Heart Advice for Difficult Times** we can open our hearts and minds beyond limit.

"To stay with the shakiness (of life) – to stay with a broken heart, with a rumbling stomach, with the feeling of hopelessness and wanting to get revenge – that is the path of true awakening. Sticking with that uncertainty, getting the knack of relaxing is the midst of chaos, learning not to panic – this is the spiritual path."

"Getting the knack of catching ourselves, of gently and compassionately catching ourselves, is the path of the warrior."

How you deal with the past coming up and how you deal with daily is in your hands.

It won't be easy and it will constantly challenge you but it's in those very moments that you can face the spiritual tests.

In moments of irritation and pain, you can stay open, curious and choose peace or choose revenge, anger and continue to stay stuck.

There's no hard and fast rules but a gentle encouragement for you to do your best and step up to the spiritual challenge in front of you.

As far as present and future relationships that will enter your life, learn to live a more enlightened and conscious person.

Operate from the place of your soul today when it comes to dating and relationships.

If you're currently living in a soul-centered place, and you've been doing the internal work, you'll show up in a certain way.

If you're showing up from an awakened soul place, you'll treat the people you date with respect, kindness and compassion.

You'll accept people for who they are and you won't try to change them.

You'll show up for the person in front of you and you won't compare them to the other people you've dated. You won't try to change them or get them to conform to your preferences. You won't demand or control them, fix or change them.

If you're coming from an awakened place, you won't have expectations of – or timelines for – future relationships. You'll let the relationship proceed at its own pace and end up in whatever format it does. You don't have to marry someone or have kids with them. You allow whatever happens to happen.

You won't put down the other person, criticize, get angry with or feel superior to any new partners.

You'll show up as your own person in the relationship, not as someone who is dependent and clingy. You're NOT going to mold your life around the other person's life or become another person so you can be compatible with your partner.

Your moods won't depend on their moods. Your behavior won't depend on their behavior. There won't be any tit-for-tat hurting of each other in this relationship. This will be an awakened relationship.

For every moment, you'll decide how to react in that moment. You won't pull back the past to skewer the person. You won't let this person's past actions – or any ex's past behavior – dictate how you respond to this person now.

You'll accept the person for who they are and you'll deal with them in the moment that's in front of you. This is a present-day, moment-to-moment relationship, not one stuck in the past.

You are a new person. You have let go of the past and are completely present for the person you're interested in today.

10. The Step of Compassion

"Our compassion towards others is limited, partial, prejudicial, and conditioned by whether we feel close to them. Genuine compassion must be unconditional." The Dalai Lama, *An Open Heart*

To deal with the anger we spoke about in previous chapters and to forgive any resentments you still have towards your ex, use the compassion step to envelop your ex with understanding, patience and acceptance.

When I left the relationship, anger and bitterness filled me. I doubt I was very compassionate; more than likely, I wanted my ex to suffer. I held a lot of anger at her for ending the relationship. I blamed her for many of the relationship's problems.

It wasn't until years later when I began to see that she might have had a point. I began to see the world from her perspective.

As difficult as it is, try to look at the world from other people's perspectives. Put yourself in their shoes. Put yourself in your ex's shoes to see what they were going through at the time of the divorce or breakup. How did they have to deal with you? How did you hurt your ex or create a dangerous situation for them?

Also, reflect on your ex's life and how they grew up; consider the baggage they walked into this world with. Consider their difficult childhood and upbringing or the people who might have hurt them along the way.

If you put yourself in their shoes and feel the pain they suffered, you'll more easily let go of the past. If you see the world through their eyes, you're less likely to be angry at them or hold resentments towards them.

During the relationship, you couldn't put yourself in their shoes, but this may be possible after some time has passed. Even if you can't put yourself in their shoes and see anything from their perspective, try to find something, anything, that helps you understand their suffering. Look at what led them to do the things they did and what made them say the things they said.

If you go behind what happened and what your ex said, seeking to consider their life story in total, everything will make sense in the grand scheme of things.

Some people say compassion is over-rated but we don't use compassion enough. It's a tool you can use on a daily basis. Create a compassion habit to put yourself in other people's shoes – including those of your ex.

Look at the similarities you shared and how you were in the same boat.

Stop judging this person; give them a break. You may believe they acted with malicious intent to harm you but…how else could they have acted? Where were they coming from? What was going on in their life? What made them do the things they did?

As I mentioned earlier, in a spiritual sense, you and everyone else are cut from the same cloth. We are all humans and we all want the same things. If you create division and barriers between you and your ex, you'll have trouble bridging the differences and moving on.

If you extend compassion to your ex by understanding where they came from, what they were going through and what it must have been like for them, you're much less likely to hold up the weapons of division. Instead, you'll pick up the tools of friendship.

Good people display challenging behaviors when life becomes stressful or when they find themselves against a wall. People with the kindest hearts and best intentions may act greedy, selfish, mean-spirited and harmful when they don't know how to cope with a situation in their life.

Put this person in an aura of light and try your best, every day, to shower them with sunlight or a golden light.

If you can't come up with compassionate thoughts and behaviors towards others, check in with yourself. Examine your own upbringing, life and thoughts. In a "me, me, me" world, we so often think about ourselves and the hurts we have suffered, we completely forget to consider other people.

How much of your day do you spend thinking about yourself? How much of your day do you fill with judgment, resentment and thoughts of your own pain?

Being mindful of your thoughts and behaviors can reveal that the root cause of division and separation is you – not what your ex did.

You can take the high road and forgive them even if what they did was unforgivable.

See the previous discussions on forgiveness and setting a daily habit of forgiveness.

When I started talking to counselors, writing about what happened and reflecting on my past, I saw the many problems I had brought to the relationship.

My thoughts changed from regarding her as an evil and malicious person to seeing that I had also caused much suffering and harm in the relationship.

I took the focus off what she did and instead looked at my own behavior and tendencies during the heated part of our marriage.

When you start looking at your own behavior, you must also start cultivating compassion for yourself.

You're not perfect either and you couldn't have figured it all out. You were doing the best you could under the circumstances. Give yourself a break; don't consider yourself to be a ruthless perpetrator who hurt those around you.

You need more compassion for yourself and others so you can heal your past relationship with your ex, as well as all your relationships. This is even necessary for world healing.

We must extend compassion and reduce judgment in all aspects of our relationships.

We must see how we are all spiritually connected with each other instead of harping on our differences and misinterpreting each other's intentions.

Not every person is greedy and malicious and out to get you; you can imagine that if you hold onto such a world-view, you will constantly feel threatened and insecure.

The golden rule is the best way to approach this. Think about others the way you want others to think about you. Talk about others the way you want others to talk about you. Treat others the way you want others to treat you. Interpret others' actions the way you want others to interpret your actions.

Instead of involving yourself in your ego, set a conscious practice to be compassionate towards others. Open your heart with kindness and love. Use spiritual and religious practices to see the good in others.

Remember that when you shift your perspective, you can shift your life. When you transform anger and resentment, you can live with more peace of mind and kindness.

Anger and resentment will keep you stuck. However, compassion will release you from the prison you've created for yourself. Compassion will liberate you and help you move on with your life.

Even if you're not extending compassion for the sake of others, you'll experience benefits when you spread compassion and live compassionately. You'll be more relaxed and peaceful.

Strive to be more compassionate and to see others in a connected spirit. Look for commonalities that reduce differences instead of disparities that build walls.

11. The Step of Strength

"There is life after failure and it can be a very satisfying life…others will learn that a broken heart is like a broken bone – it hurts terribly but it heals, and as has been suggested, it often heals stronger at the broken place." Harold Kushner, *Overcoming Life's Disappointments*

After my divorce, I saw no hope for better days in the future.

It looked bleak, grim and dark. I felt that all my happiest days were behind me and that I was crushed. There was no more hope for the future.

I've since found this to not be true. In fact, my happiest, most fulfilling days are in the present.

It feels like the marriage was unduly suffocating and painful to me.

What appears to be the case can sometimes be the opposite. It's a matter of perspective.

You may feel like the end of your relationship is the worst thing possible, but you could be welcoming in the best period of your life – one of peace, happiness and fulfillment. The end of your relationship could lead you to peace of mind and calmness. It could lead you to another relationship and happiness.

There's nothing wrong with a broken heart, as Harold Kushner points out in his quote above. In fact, you can become stronger in the place where you break down.

Reflect upon all the hard moments in your life. All the defining moments were likely the difficult ones.

If you struggled in an area of school, you likely excelled in it later or went on to major in it.

If you were bad at basketball or baseball, you likely worked harder to the point that you became better at it.

If you experienced the loss of a loved one, their passing likely inspired or motivated you in some significant way.

Your life's greatest pains have become – and can continue to be – your life's greatest joys.

The question then becomes, how do you use this pain and heartbreak to your advantage?

How do you change this painful breakup from your weakness to your strength?

How do you change this from something that holds you back to something that moves you forward?

The step of strength requires that you remember you've done this over and over.

You've overcome every great setback and obstacle. You've found a way to deal with every challenge you've confronted.

So, note to self: You are in the business of overcoming the past and breaking through the obstacles in your way.

You've lost people and relationships before. You've let go of them before. If you've done it once, you can do it again.

You have the experience to let go of the past.

You cultivate the strength to let go by confronting the past whenever it arises. You allow the memories and sentimental feelings to show up but you don't run away from them.

You allow the past to sit with you and be present in your life. Then you show the past to the door.

It may not be easy to do this every time – to turn these memories into physical scenarios in which you visualize pain entering your home and then yourself escorting out those painful memories.

You cultivate strength by doing this every time. It's easier to sit and partake of all the good memories and all your ex's virtues. The courage part involves consciously letting go of these memories.

If you were operating by default and allowed your mind to rule your life, you would simply embrace past thoughts and memories.

You may have to remove thoughts and feelings from your proverbial house every day.

Do not act like a polite homeowner towards memories of your ex. Instead, show the over-staying thoughts and feelings to the door.

If you were dormant and acted by default thinking, these thoughts and feelings would consume your life and stay forever.

After confronting your thoughts, you must engage your body and your physical being in letting go.

Letting go doesn't happen by sleeping and pushing the covers over your head to hide from the world.

I get it. I was there.

You think going anywhere is too much hassle and embarrassment. You want to sit home and stew in the sadness and pain. However, the longer you do this, the longer it's going to take to move on.

As much as you don't want to do it, now is the time to get physical.

Not exercise, necessarily, but simply staying active, staying engaged and participating in some routine activities outside the house.

I know we talked in an earlier chapter about going within and doing the inner work, but not to the point of the work becoming simply grieving and feeling sorry for yourself.

You do need alone time to go within and figure things out but you also need a connection to the outside world.

You need friends, dinners and other parts of your old life that resemble a normal life.

The idea isn't to become a recluse and suffer in misery by yourself.

It's to live a balanced life – some down time for you to go within and some social time to get away from yourself and be in the world around you.

Doing old activities, going out and interacting with others is the key to moving on.

If you fall into the habit of crying by yourself for hours in your locked room or apartment, you will have trouble moving on.

Strength requires you to stand strong when you want to hide and run away.

When you feel like throwing in the towel and becoming a hot, boiling soup of misery and suffering, grab yourself.

Check your thoughts. Watch your emotions. Live your life.

Engage thoughts, emotions and body so you're not spiraling into a sad and tragic place.

Remind yourself that you've done it before; others (divorcing couples and broken-up pairs) have gone on to find happiness and love afterwards.

I hope you believe me when I tell you that I am 100 times happier today than when I was married. My life contains so much freedom, joy and happiness.

I tell you this not because I want to show you how great my life is now but to remind you of how far I've come from a place where I didn't want to live anymore.

I'm certain that if this was my experience, it will likely be your experience too. The only question you're going to ask yourself now is why you didn't call off the relationship sooner.

No matter how sad, dark and gloomy your world may feel and look right now, it will get better.

You must trust that good things are coming your way.

12. The Step of Trust

"We may not always understand what is happening to us, or to another, or what is occurring in a particular situation; but if we trust ourselves, or another, or we place our trust in a process or an ideal, we can find a powerful stabilizing element embracing security, balance, and openness within the trusting which, in some way, if not based on naiveté, intuitively guides us and protects us from harm or self-destruction." Jon Kabat-Zinn, *Wherever You Go, There You Are*

The final step is trusting.

Yes, letting go requires trust.

Have you ever been on a trapeze, for example, or played on the monkey bars on a school playground?

Or encountered any situation in which you've had to let go of one thing to grab onto something else?

When you must let go and grab onto something else, not knowing whether you'll land at the next place, you exercise some degree of trust.

You're counting on the next island, the next bar, the next trapeze swing to be waiting for you when you let go.

Will you know with 100% certainty it's going to appear? You won't.

Will it likely appear? Yes.

Will this require some degree of trust?

Indeed.

I'm going to speak about trusting in three contexts and help you develop trust in each of these scenarios.

First, you'll have to trust in letting go of the past, even if you can't see it or aren't quite there.

You may never believe you're going to get over your ex or your past. You may never have any hope in the future. The only way to get from the place where you are to the place where you'd like to be is trust.

I've given you many reasons to trust the process in this book. First, trust your own personal experiences; know that you've come out of your darkest places and your most difficult personal challenges. Know that others have done it, too; people have come out of bad relationships and been able to move on.

If you need more proof or hope, know that I am another real-life example of someone who did.

I thought my whole world crumbled and there was no point in living, yet I got through these chapters of my life and came out on the other side. It took work but it was possible.

You don't just wake up one day and find yourself "over" it. It's not as black and white as that. It's not a quick run through grief and recovery.

Maybe some people get over things and move on quickly when life's challenges arise but this isn't all of us. I doubt it's the people reading this book, right?!

I went through all these steps of letting go and made it. I'm here to shout that if you're on the other side of letting go, take a leap.

Do the work. Follow the steps and you'll get there.

Many millions of people have done it before you, reminding you that it's possible. People who have lost their loved ones through torture or other horrific ways of leaving the world have also found ways in their life to let go.

Believe that letting go is possible.

Next, you're going to have to trust yourself to get through this experience, to survive and thrive.

Yes, you're not only going to get through this experience, you're going to come out even stronger than before.

Because of this experience, you'll be better at handling life.

Because of this experience, you'll make wiser decisions about people and relationships.

Because of this experience, you'll get better at handling change and dealing with whatever comes your way.

This experience will fundamentally alter your life and your character for the better.

Some experiences affect and change us a little bit.

If this breakup or former relationship has rocked your world, be prepared for awareness, understanding, guidance and decision-making to also rock your world.

In every way you experience a negative effect, you'll encounter positive effects in the form of the lessons and understanding you get out of the experience.

I've also found that as far back as you're able to fall, you can move the same distance forward.

Yes, the farther back this experience takes you and breaks you down, the more you must grow and develop as a person. As much as you're suffering and hurting, you have opened the space to welcome in joy and happiness.

The pain created the crater of sadness and despair.

Eventually, through the necessary work, this crater will evaporate and become empty.

In its place, you will receive the joys and rewards of experience and of having overcome sadness.

You will receive all the good things you want. You will receive the right partner and the right relationship.

You must trust that good things are coming your way, in the very near future.

Life, like the stock market, goes in cycles.

Sometimes life pushes you down and sometimes the waves make you ride high across the world.

Sometimes you get everything you want and sometime you get everything you don't want.

A difficult breakup will set you up for making better decisions, finding better partners and dealing with the future emotions of a relationship.

The end of this relationship is making you better at relationships and better at making decisions.

You can choose to see bad relationships as bad decision-making on your part or…

you can see your relationships as representing your ability to grow, mature and make wiser decisions.

You went through bad relationships and incompatible people to learn who the right person is for you.

When we make mistakes or experience failures, we tend to make better decisions the next time.

Many of us learn what went wrong and then course correct; we don't make the same mistake again.

I am asking you to trust your ability to learn from mistakes and make improvements, as you've likely done in every other area of your life.

If you become more self-aware, understand relationships better, do the inner work and are more careful about the partners you select, you'll find a relationship you truly desire.

If you do the work and take heed of past lessons, things will work out for you.

You must look at the people in your life who have gone through hardship and heartbreak, gotten through it and come out stronger in the end.

You must focus on people who might have fallen hard but who got back up and entered relationships that were fulfilling and joyful.

I follow a handful of personalities in the entertainment world; many of them fail and falter but eventually get it right.

Television talk show host Steve Harvey was with incompatible people until he met the love of his life. It was someone he had known previously but he didn't realize how good she was for him until he had gone through some bad relationships.

Actor Ashton Kutcher was in relationships that didn't work out and even had a short-lived marriage; then he met Mila Kunis. They have since had a child, gotten married and, as of 2018, are together.

Hollywood may be a terrible example of moving on but you do know of many celebrities who lost at love, then found love in their second, third, fourth or fifth tries.

They had to trust that the future would be better than the past. They had to let go just like you must let go now.

Aarti (light)

"The wound is the place where the light enters you." Rumi

When you walk out of these 12 steps of letting go, you will likely feel exhausted and tired.

You've just come through a burning but now there is light.

In the Indian tradition, at the end of many rituals, we light an oil lamp with a cotton wick. We put the lamp on a metal plate as we sing devotional songs to the higher powers. The priest circulates the plate to the highest powers, then to those in attendance.

This is a ritual after the prayers, after the homa or the burning of symbolic items into the air.

After the prayers, rituals and blessings, there is this aarti ritual, which circulates light.

After the work, there is light.

Your burning will take work; I've described this work in the 12 steps above.

Now I'm going to encourage you to actually take those steps.

I needed each of those steps to move on but I took them during different parts of my healing.

You don't have to do it all at once and you don't have to do it in order.

You don't have to start until you're ready. However, if you are sick and tired of letting the past hold you back, these steps will come into play.

On some levels, much of this is internal, so you really don't have to do any of it.

You may think you'll just contemplate these 12 steps and then receive their benefits.

Unfortunately, that won't happen.

You won't be able to move on until you take these steps.

If you decide to move on without letting go, you will remain stuck in your past relationships. If you don't let go once and for all, resistance and the same patterns will arise in your future relationships.

You know the steps; your duty now is to take them for yourself – for who you are now and in the future.

You no longer have to let the past punish you.

You're not a bad person and you didn't commit a crime.

You're not a terrible person who is the victim of someone else's actions.

You had a life experience, a relationship that didn't work out.

The relationship may have ended badly, violently and cruelly but the only disservice to your life is if you chose to remain stuck in this place.

If you stay stuck, your ex continues to have an undue amount of influence over your life.

Your children see that you can't move on from this life challenge. This cripples their ability to move on from future life obstacles themselves.

You want to show them that you can face the darkness, burn and come out in the light.

You may be getting a lot of information and advice from everyday people who have your best interests at heart. Much of what they tell you is true about healing heartbreak, recovering from splits and moving on from divorce.

Well, except for those people who tell you to simply get over it. They have no idea what they're talking about.

The other folks have likely gone down similar paths. They have found strategies that worked, and have moved on and found happiness.

Listen to them.

Their words and advice are likely in one of the 12 steps I've described.

These 12 steps stem from spiritual principles that various thought leaders and spiritual teachers have shared.

If your friends can't provide the instructions for letting go, tap into the powers of the divine guides and teachers.

The people who have tapped into the spiritual world have a message for you, too.

I've shared a few nuggets of wisdom from a dozen spiritual leaders – each with a different step and angle for moving forward.

Each has their own books, courses, seminars and teachings on how to take advantage and go further in every step.

You can pick up those books, follow their teachings and become a monk or nun yourself!

Or you can use their wisdom as guidance to get past this obstacle in your life, to free yourself and go after the life that's waiting for you. Go after the love and relationships you were meant to have.

Again, life has burned you, but after the burning is light.

There is aarti, which is light but also clarity, understanding, awareness, wisdom and knowledge.

You have now received the burning's gifts.

You can move forward as a much stronger, wiser and more resilient person in all areas of your life.

Learning to let go of a relationship will teach you to let go of other areas of your life as well.

After you've done the work, you'll take with you these invaluable lessons and steps to conquer other areas of your life.

Our time on this journey is over, friends, but I'll see you out there in the battlefield of life.

Let's walk together through any other hardships or soul-crushing circumstances that come our way.

Our lives may face disruptions, and circumstances may alter our plans, but after the burning we will emerge as the people we were meant to be.

We will shine and walk in the light. We will become guardians of the light and guide the light for others. Together, we will show others the way when they are stuck in the past.

It's been a pleasure sharing this journey with you.

I wish you continued "letting go" and transformation.

With much courage and light to move on.

Your friend, Vishnu

*If you enjoyed this book and believe it helped you, please consider leaving a review on the Amazon page under a *Leave a Customer Review*, so others will be able to find and appreciate this book also.

References

"For a seed to achieve its greatest expression, it must come completely undone. The shell cracks, its insides come out and everything changes. To someone who doesn't understand growth, it would look like complete destruction." Cynthia Occelli

Deepak Chopra, *Spiritual Solutions: Answers to Life's Greatest Challenges*, New York, Harmony Books, 2012

Eckhart Tolle, *A New Earth: Awakening to Your Life's Purpose*, New York, The Penguin Group, 2005

Gary Zukav, *Soul to Soul; Communications from the Heart*, New York, Free Press, 2007

Harold Kushner, *Overcoming Life's Disappointments*, New York, Alfred Knopf, 2006

John Kabat-Zinn, *Wherever You Go There You Are: Mindfulness Meditation in Everyday Life*, New York, Hyperion, 1994

Pema Chodron, *When Things Fall Apart: Heart Advice for Difficult Times*, Boulder, CO, Shambala Publication Inc, 1997

Ram Dass, *Polishing the Mirror: How to Live from Your Spiritual Heart*, Boulder, Co, Sound True, 2013

Ram Dass, *Paths to God; Living the Bhagavad Gita*, New York, Harmony Books, 2004

The Dalai Lama, *An Open Heart: Practicing Compassion in Everyday Life*, Boston, Little, Brown & Company, 2001

Thich Nhat Hanh, *Essential Writings*, New York, Orbis Books, 2001

Thic Nhat Hanh, *Fear: Essential Wisdom for Getting Through the Storm*, New York, HarperOne, 2012

About the Author

Vishnu of Vishnu's Virtues is the author of *The Self Romance Manifesto: 21 Practices to End Self Hate and Invite Love In, 10 Sacred Laws of Healing a Broken Heart,* and *Is God Listening?*

He is the blogger behind the popular relationship and personal growth blog, *Vishnu's Virtues,* where he writes about overcoming heartbreak, letting go of the past and moving on.

Vishnu also coaches people on starting over and rebuilding their lives after difficult transitions like divorces and breakups. He helps people overcome past relationships, trust themselves more and find new love in their lives. He coaches people to open their hearts to love again and find a compatible life partner.

Before writing and coaching, Vishnu practiced divorce and family law. While he enjoyed helping people navigate the justice system, it wasn't his true life's purpose. Vishnu left the law field and pursued his calling to help others find love after challenging relationships and heartbreak.

To keep up with Vishnu's weekly posts and for a free guide on opening your heart to love, please visit his blog at www.vishnusvirtues.com.

For the Vishnu's Virtues blog:
www.vishnusvirtues.com

Vishnu on Facebook:
https://www.facebook.com/vishnusvirtues/

Vishnu on Twitter:
https://twitter.com/VishnusVirtues

Vishnu on Instagram:
https://www.instagram.com/vishnusvirtues/

Vishnu on Amazon:
https://www.amazon.com/Vishnus-Virtues/e/B00XH077L0

For constructive feedback or questions, email me at
vishnusvirtues@gmail.com

Made in the USA
Coppell, TX
05 April 2021